Draw It!

Sports Stars

by Tiffany Peterson
illustrations by David Westerfield

Heinemann Library
Chicago, Illinois

Chicago, IL 60002

Customer Service 888-454-2279
Visit our website at www.heinemannlibrary.com

Designed by Depke Design
Illustrated by David Westerfield
Photograph p. 4 by Kimberly Saar
Printed and bound in the United States by Lake Book Manufacturing, Inc.

06 05 04 03
10 9 8 7 6 5 4 3 2 1

Library of Congress Cataloging-in-Publication Data
Peterson, Tiffany.
  Sports stars / Tiffany Peterson; illustrations by David Westerfield.
      p. cm. -- (Draw it!)
Summary: Presents instructions for drawing famous male and female
athletes from a variety of sports, including tennis, basketball, and golf.
Includes bibliographical references and index.
  ISBN 1-4034-0213-2 (HC), 1-4034-4032-8 (Pbk)
  1. Sports in art--Juvenile literature. 2. Drawing--Technique--Juvenile
literature. [1. Sports in art. 2. Drawing--Technique.] I. Westerfield, David,
1956- ill. II. Title. III. Series.
  NC825.S62P47 2003
  743'.89796--dc21
                                    2002015491

Some words are shown in bold, **like this.** You can
find out what they mean by looking in the glossary.

Contents

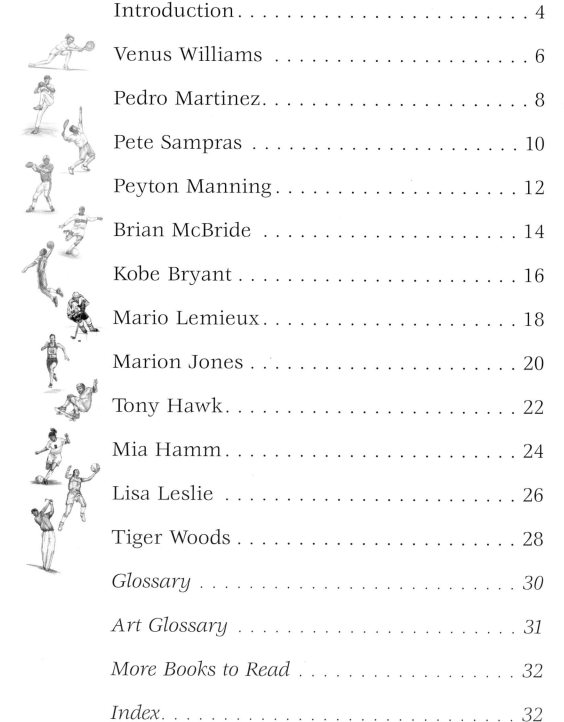

Introduction

Would you like to improve the pictures that you draw?

Well, you can! In this book, the artist has drawn some of your favorite pictures. He has used lines and shapes to draw each picture in small, simple steps. Follow these steps and your picture will come together for you too.

Here is advice from the artist:

- Always draw lightly at first.

- Draw all the shapes and pieces in the right places.

- Pay attention to the spaces between the lines as well as the lines themselves.

- Add details and **shading** to finish your drawing.

- And finally, erase the lines you don't need.

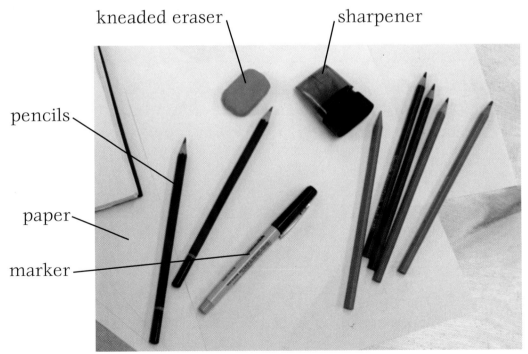

You only need a few supplies to get started.

There are just four things you need for drawing:

- a pencil (medium or soft). You might also use a fine marker or pen to finish your drawing.
- a pencil sharpener.
- paper.
- an eraser. A **kneaded eraser** works best. It can be squeezed into small or odd shapes. This eraser can also make pencil lines lighter without erasing them.

Now, are you ready? Do you have everything? Then turn the page and let's draw!

*The drawings in this book were done by David Westerfield. David started drawing when he was very young. In college, he studied drawing and painting. Now he is a **commercial artist** who owns his own graphic design business. He has two children, and he likes to draw with them. David's advice to anyone who hopes to become an artist is to "practice, practice, practice–and learn as much as you can from other artists."*

Draw Venus Williams

Richard Williams coached his daughters, Venus and Serena, at tennis. Both have become great players. Venus was the first African-American woman to win Wimbledon since Althea Gibson in 1957 and 1958.

1 **Sketch** a **horizontal** oval. Add a larger, slanted oval.

2 Draw an **angled** line from the bottom oval as a **guideline** for the leg. Add a circle for the knee and an oval for the foot. Draw an upside down L coming from the right of the bottom oval. Add a circle for the knee and a foot shape at the bottom. Draw circles at the top of the slanted oval for the shoulders. Add an angled line for the left arm and a straight line for the right arm. Add circles for the elbows and hands.

3 Sketch a pointed oval for the head. Draw lines across the face as guidelines for the eyes, nose, and mouth. Sketch a circle for the racquet. Add a curved triangle for the handle.

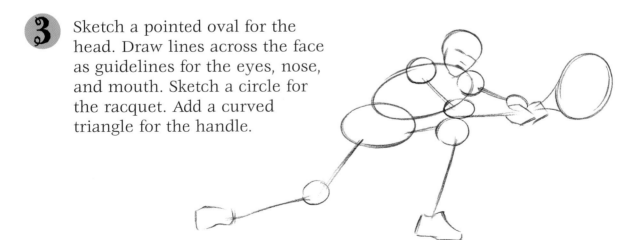

4 Fill in the shape of the body by drawing lines connecting the guideline circles.

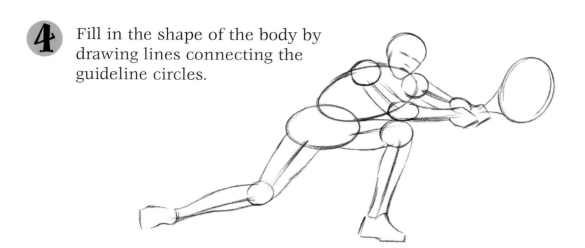

5 Sketch the tennis shoes. Draw the outline for the tennis dress. Add some lines to show the folds in the material. Draw two lines around the front wrist for a wristband. Draw eyes and eyebrows. Add the nose and curved lines on each side. Draw the mouth and ear. Draw many curvy lines for hair.

6 Erase the guidelines that you don't need. Darken the lines of the drawing. Add lines in the racket for the strings and a circle for the tennis ball. Add some more lines in the dress for folds. Add horizontal lines above the ankles for socks. **Shade** the arms, legs, and face. Add shading for a shadow.

Draw Pedro Martinez

As a boy, Pedro Martinez played baseball with anything round, even his sisters' dolls' heads. The Los Angeles Dodgers discovered him at age 15. He and his older brother Ramon played together for the Dodgers in 1992 and 1993. In 1999, they played together again, for the Boston Red Sox.

1 **Sketch** a **vertical** oval on top of a **horizontal** oval.

2 Draw two small circles on the top oval's right side. Connect them with a straight line and a slanted line for **guidelines** for an arm. Lightly sketch a shape like a sideways teardrop as a guideline for the baseball mitt. Sketch a slanted V shape for the other arm. Add a circle at the bottom of the V for the elbow. Draw a backward 7 for the raised leg. Add a circle for the knee and a foot shape. Draw a long vertical line from the horizontal oval for the standing leg. Add a circle for the knee and a foot shape at the bottom.

3 Sketch an oval for the head. Connect it to the body with two lines. Draw three lines across the face as guidelines for the eyes, nose, and mouth. Add details like fingers to the baseball mitt.

4 Fill in the shape of the body by drawing lines connecting the guideline circles.

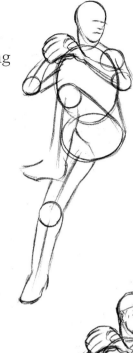

5 Sketch a half circle on top of the head and a curved line over the forehead for a baseball cap. Add the ear and a curved line for the jaw. Draw eyes, eyebrows, nose, and mouth. Draw the top of a rectangle for the tongue of the lifted shoe. Sketch the folds in the pants. Add a vertical line down the chest.

6 Erase the guidelines you no longer need. Darken lines, the bottom shoe, uniform sleeves, and most of the cap. Draw a white B shape on the cap front. Lightly **shade** the pants, raised shoe, and baseball glove. Add shoelaces and other details. Lightly shade the face. Write "BOSTON" across the jersey. Sketch a horizontal line behind Pedro's lower foot for the mound, and another line above that for the horizon.

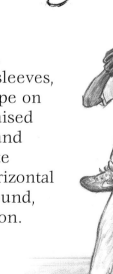

Draw Pete Sampras

When he was young, Pete Sampras found a tennis racket in his basement and practiced hitting a ball against the wall for hours. When his family moved from Washington, D.C., to California, Pete could play tennis more. At age 19, he won the U.S. Open, the youngest man ever to do so.

1 **Sketch** a circle and an oval connected by a short curved line.

2 Draw two smaller circles on the big circle as **guidelines** for the shoulders. Add circles for the elbows. Draw lines connecting the elbows to the shoulders, and lines from the elbows. Sketch rough hand shapes. Draw two **angled** lines for legs. Add circles for the knees. Draw rough foot shapes at the end of the lines.

3 Draw a circle for the head and connect it to the body with a short curved line. Add the jaw. Draw guidelines for the eyes, nose, and mouth. Draw a curved line for the neck. Add a spoon shape for the tennis racket.

4 Fill in the shape of the body by drawing lines that connect the guideline circles. Add fingers to the hands. Draw curved lines for the tops of the tennis shoes.

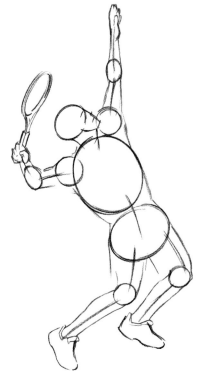

5 Draw a curved line for the top of the shorts. Finish the shorts. Add the shirt. Sketch in some lines on the shirt for folds. Add a curved rectangle along the neck for the collar. Add the ear and the hairline. Add an eyebrow and an eye. Draw the nose and the mouth. Add **shading** under the chin.

6 Erase the guidelines you no longer need. Add shading on the arms, legs, and face. Darken the hair. Add shading in the shirt. Darken the tennis racket and add lines for the strings. Add shading under Pete's feet for a shadow.

Draw Peyton Manning

Peyton Manning's father was a professional football quarterback, and Peyton decided to be one, too. In college, he was runner-up for the Heisman Trophy. He is the first University of Tennessee football player ever to have his number **retired.**

1 **Sketch** two ovals as **guidelines** for the body.

2 Sketch two **angled** lines for guidelines for the legs. Add circles for the knees. Draw an oval for one foot and a foot shape for the other. Draw a circle for the shoulder on the right side of the top oval. Add an angled line for the arm. Draw a circle for the elbow and the rough shape of the hand. Add the other arm by drawing a circle for the shoulder and an angled line with a circle for the elbow. Draw an oval for the football in Peyton's hand.

3 Sketch an oval with a flat top and a pointed bottom for Peyton's face. Connect the face to the body with two lines. Draw a half of a circle around the face for the helmet. Draw lines in the face to show where the eyes, nose, and mouth will go.

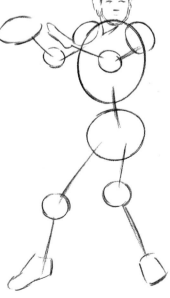

4 Fill in the shape of the body by drawing lines connecting the guideline circles. Add a curved line across the waist.

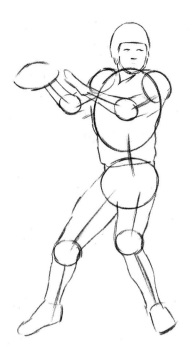

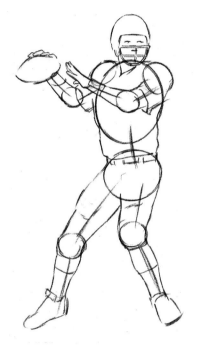

5 Add two **horizontal** lines and one **vertical** line across the face for the **facemask.** Draw a J around the upper arm for the sleeve. Add curved lines around the wrists for wristbands. Add fingers. Draw a line for the other sleeve. Add some lines in the **jersey** for folds in the material. Draw a sideways hook shape for the pad on the right leg. Sketch part of a rectangle for the left leg pad. Add curved lines for the socks.

6 Erase the guidelines you no longer need. Draw the number 18 on the sleeve and on the jersey's front behind Peyton's arm. Add lines on the pants and helmet. Draw a curved line across the football. Add **shading** to the legs, the jersey, and the football. Draw a stripe and rectangle on top of the helmet. Darken the edge of Peyton's face. Draw eyebrows, eyes, nose, and mouth. Add shading under Peyton's feet for a shadow.

Draw Brian McBride

Every morning as a boy, no matter what day it was, Brian McBride practiced soccer. He **dribbled** the ball around trees, juggled it on his knees and feet, and practiced goal shots. He says, "If you love the game, you'll become a better player."

1 **Sketch** a circle and an oval. Connect them with a short curved line.

2 Draw a long curved line for the right leg. Draw a circle for the knee and another circle for the foot. Draw a V for the other leg with a circle at the bottom of the V for the knee. Add an oval for the foot. Draw circles for the shoulders. Sketch an **angled** line for the right arm and a curved line for the left arm. Add circles for elbows and ovals for hands.

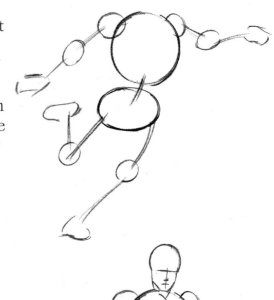

3 Sketch an oval for the head. Add two short, vertical lines for the neck. Draw a T as a **guideline** for the eyes, nose, and mouth.

4 Fill in the shape of the body by drawing lines connecting the guideline circles.

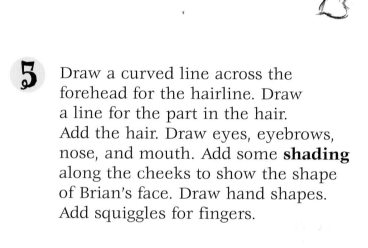

5 Draw a curved line across the forehead for the hairline. Draw a line for the part in the hair. Add the hair. Draw eyes, eyebrows, nose, and mouth. Add some **shading** along the cheeks to show the shape of Brian's face. Draw hand shapes. Add squiggles for fingers.

6 Sketch the **jersey.** Add two curved lines across each wrist for sleeves. Draw a curved rectangle for the left collar. Add the rough shape of the other collar. Draw two lines across the jersey. Sketch curved lines across the legs and the waist for the shorts. Write 26 on the jersey and the shorts. Add curved lines across the ankles for the tops of the shoes. Add shading to the jersey and shorts. Draw a circle for the soccer ball.

Draw Kobe Bryant

Kobe Bryant and his basketball team, the Los Angeles Lakers, won NBA championships for three straight years, starting in 2000. Kobe has broken records set by great basketball players like Wilt Chamberlain.

1 **Sketch** a long oval and a circle. Connect them with a curved line.

2 Draw circles for the shoulders. Add two curved lines for arms. Add circles for the elbows and **crescent** shapes for the hands. Draw an L shape for the right leg. Add a circle for the knee. Sketch a rough foot shape. Draw an **angled** line for the left leg. Add a circle for the knee and a rough foot shape.

3 Sketch a circle with a half-oval shape at the bottom for the head. Add a curved line for the neck. Draw a short line for an eyeline. Draw a circle for a basketball in Kobe's hand.

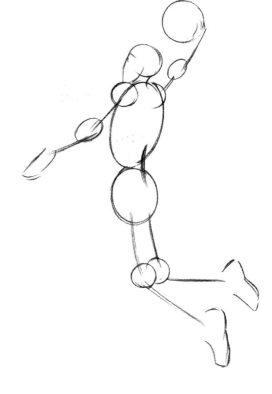

4 Fill in the shape of the body by drawing lines connecting the **guideline** circles. Add the shapes of the fingers to the hands.

5 Draw curvy lines for the shorts. The bottom edge has a notch like an upside-down V. Add a curvy stripe down the side of the shorts. Draw a half circle around the front shoulder for the armhole in the **jersey**. Add a curvy stripe along the side of the jersey.

6 Erase the guidelines you no longer need. Draw Kobe's mouth open by drawing a half circle. Sketch the ear. Add a wavy line for the hairline. Sketch the eye, eyebrow, and nose. Add two curved lines across the top of Kobe's arm for an armband. Darken lines of the drawing. Color in the stripe on the side of the uniform. Write Bryant and the number 8 on the back of the jersey. Color the hair. Add **shading** to the face, the front arm, and the legs. Add details to the shoes and the basketball.

Draw Mario Lemieux

Mario Lemieux grew up admiring the players on professional hockey's Montreal Canadiens. His father poured an ice rink in their yard so Mario could practice anytime. He grew up to play professional hockey and became known as "Super Mario."

1 **Sketch** two overlapping ovals as **guidelines** for the body.

2 Draw a backward L for the right arm. Add a circle inside of the bend in the L. Put a slanted rectangle to the lower left of the circle for the right glove. To start the left arm draw a vertical line with a circle at the end. Add another slanted rectangle below that circle for the left glove. Draw a slanted line from the left edge of the bottom oval for a leg guideline. Draw a line from the right edge of the same oval for the right leg guideline. Add a circle for the right knee. Add ovals for the shapes of the skates.

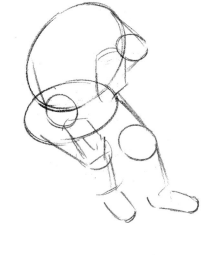

3 Sketch a circle with a half oval under it for the helmet and Mario's face. Draw eyes, nose, and mouth. Add a curvy line across the helmet.

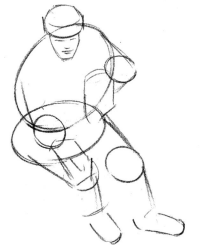

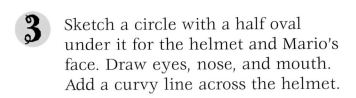

4 Sketch a rough sideways V on the side of the **jersey.** Add a stripe from the V across the shoulders. Create a V-shaped neckline. Finish the left arm. Draw several curved lines across the legs just under the knees for the socks. Add a hockey stick. Draw curvy lines for stripes on the lower part of the jersey.

5 Sketch the thick gloves. Make a loop for the thumb on each glove. Finish the outline of the skates. Make the top of the skate wider than the bottom. Sketch laces in the skates. Add a small V for each skate's **blade.** Draw a rectangle with a curved line on top for the hockey **puck.**

6 Erase the guidelines you no longer need. Darken the lines of the drawing. Color the shorts. Add **shading** to the jersey, face, helmet, and legs. Sketch a penguin on the front of the jersey and color it. Darken the front of the hockey stick. Write 66 on the sleeves of the jersey. Add some shading under the hockey stick and under Mario's legs and feet for shadows on the ice.

Draw Marion Jones

Marion Jones watched her first Olympics at age 9. The winners' excitement made her want to win Olympic medals. In the 2000 Olympics, she competed in 5 events. She won 3 gold and 2 bronze medals to reach her goal.

1 **Sketch** two ovals as **guidelines** for the body. Connect them with a short curved line.

2 Sketch a short **angled** line from the bottom oval. Add a circle for the knee. Draw a vertical line from the circle ending with a triangle shape for the foot. Sketch a curved line for the top of the left leg. Add a sideways foot shape.

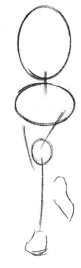

3 Sketch a pointed oval for the face and head. Lightly draw guidelines for the eyes, nose, and mouth. Draw two curved lines for the neck. Sketch two **vertical** lines in the neck. Draw two circles for shoulders. Draw a very narrow V for the left arm. Draw a circle at the point for the elbow. Add a claw-like shape for the hand. Sketch an angled line for the right arm. Draw a circle at the corner for the elbow. Sketch another claw-like shape for the right hand.

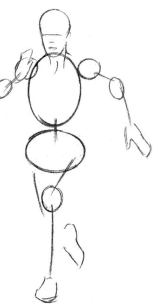

4 Fill in the shape of the body by drawing lines connecting the guideline circles. Add fingers to the hands.

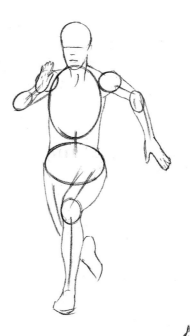

5 Draw eyes, eyebrows, nose, and mouth. Sketch a half oval for the shirt's neckline. Draw curved lines for armholes. Add a square on the front of the **jersey.** Draw a **horizontal** line just below the square for the shirt's bottom edge. Draw a curved line for the waist. Add a curved line across each of the legs to finish the shorts.

6 Erase the guidelines you no longer need. Sketch the hairline and darken the hair. Color the shirt and shorts. Leave a white stripe down the side of the shirt. **Shade** the face, neck, arms, stomach, and legs. Draw a curved line across the toes of the shoes. Write the number 102 on the shirt. Darken lines and add shading under Marion's feet for a shadow.

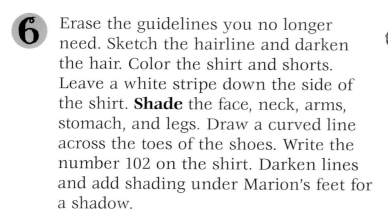

Draw Tony Hawk

When Tony Hawk was young, he had more energy than he knew what to do with. His brother gave him a skateboard when he was 9. He loved skateboarding immediately. At the age of only 14, he became a professional skateboarder.

1 **Sketch** two overlapping ovals.

2 Add a circle on top of the upper oval for the shoulder. Draw another circle and connect them with a line. Draw a short **vertical** line with a claw-like shape at the end for a hand. Where the two big ovals overlap, draw a **horizontal** line from the left with a circle at the end for the knee. Draw a vertical line for the front leg. Add a triangle at the end for the foot. Draw a vertical line for the right leg **guideline** with a foot shape at the end. Draw two angled **parallel** lines for the back arm. Add an oval for a rough hand shape.

3 Sketch a circle and a half oval for the head and face. For the helmet sketch a half circle. Add guidelines for the eyes, nose, and mouth. Draw the neck.

4 Fill in the shape of the body by drawing lines connecting the guideline circles. Sketch a long, wavy oval that comes to a point at one end for the skateboard. Add a curved line under the skateboard for a guideline for the hand. Draw the shapes of fingers to the hands. Add a V below the raised hand for the sleeve cuff.

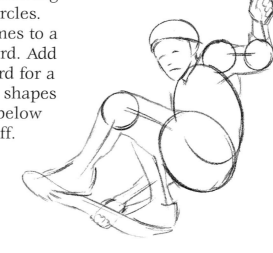

5 Sketch a small L for the nose. Draw eyes, eyebrows, the mouth, and lines on the face. Add a knee pad and elbow pad. Sketch in the shape of Tony's shirt and shorts. Add some light curved lines for the folds in the material. Draw curved lines for the tops of the shoes and socks. Sketch details on the shoes.

6 Erase the guidelines you no longer need. Darken the lines of the drawing. Add **shading** along the knee, legs, arms, and face. Add two small circles to the top of the helmet. Add circles for the wheels of the skateboard.

Draw Mia Hamm

Mia Hamm is known worldwide as one of the greatest soccer players. Winning is so important to her that when she was young, she quit during sports games if a loss appeared likely. Once she discovered her love for soccer, though, she never quit again.

1 **Sketch** a circle and a rounded rectangle. Draw a curved line through the two shapes.

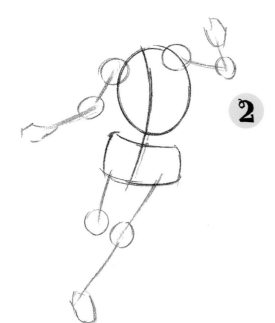

2 Draw a sideways L for the right arm. Add circles for the shoulder, elbow, and hand. Draw an **angled** line for the left arm. Add circles for the shoulder and elbow. Add a half-moon shape for the hand. Draw a long line for the right leg. Add a circle for the knee and an oval for the foot. Draw a short line for the top half of the left leg. Add a circle at the end for the knee.

3 Sketch a half circle connected to a rounded L for the head. Sketch a curved line across the face for an eyeline. Add a short, curved line for the neck.

4 Draw a curved line across the forehead for the hairline. Draw several lines from the **temple** toward the back of the head for pulled-back hair. Sketch a squiggly line in the rough shape of an oval for her ponytail. Draw an eye, eyebrow, nose, and mouth. Add the **forearms** and fingers. Fill in the legs. Draw a curved line below the knee for the top of Mia's sock. Sketch the shoe.

5 Draw some wavy and curved lines around the **guidelines** for the shirt and shorts. Add curved lines for the neck and for the shirtsleeves. Draw two curved lines at the waist. Add some lines in the shirt and across the legs of the shorts to show folds.

6 Erase the guidelines you no longer need. Darken lines. Write 9 on the **jersey** and color it. **Shade** the bottom of the shirt, the arms, the legs, and the shoe. Draw a circle for the soccer ball. Shade one side of the ball and add angled lines for **seams.** Add some shading under Mia for a shadow.

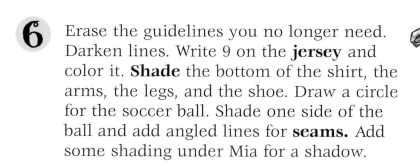

Draw Lisa Leslie

In junior high, Lisa Leslie was embarrassed by her height of six feet. A friend told her she should play basketball. She tried it and loved it. Now at 6 feet 5 inches, she plays professional basketball for the Los Angeles Sparks.

1 **Sketch** a circle and a rounded rectangle. Draw a short **vertical** line connecting them.

2 Sketch an L for the left arm and a slightly **angled** line for the right arm. Draw circles for the shoulders and elbows. Add a claw shape for the left hand and a pointed oval for the right hand. Draw two angled lines for the legs. Add circles for the knees. Sketch rough foot shapes.

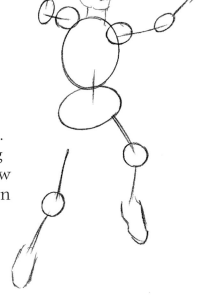

3 Sketch an oval with a flat bottom for the head. Draw three light lines across the face showing where the eyes, nose, and mouth will go. Draw two curved lines for the neck. Draw a circle on top of the right hand for the basketball.

4 Fill in the shape of the body by drawing lines connecting the **guideline** shapes. Draw the fingers.

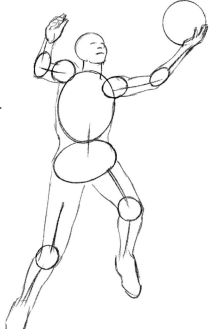

5 Draw eyes, eyebrows, nose and open mouth. Darken the bottom half of the mouth to define the top teeth. Draw curved lines for the neck of the **jersey** and for the armholes. Sketch a line across the waist. Draw wavy lines to show the folds in the material of the jersey. Draw curved lines across the tops of the legs for shorts. Add curved lines across the calves for the socks. Add details to the shoes.

6 Erase the guidelines you no longer need. Darken lines. Color the hair. Add **shading** to the arms, legs, and neck. Draw curved lines on the basketball. Write Sparks 9 on the jersey. Draw a dark stripe down the side of the uniform. Add wavy lines on the jersey and the shorts for folds in the material.

Draw Tiger Woods

Eldrick "Tiger" Woods has been playing golf since he was two years old. A **prodigy** of golf, he played in his first professional tournament in 1991, when he was only 16.

1 **Sketch** a **vertical** oval and a **horizontal** oval. Connect them with a long curved line.

2 Sketch a long, slightly curved line as a **guideline** for the right leg and an **angled** line for the left leg. Add circles for the knees. Add a rounded triangle for the right foot and a rectangle for the left foot. Sketch a backward L shape for the right arm and a straight line for the left arm. Add circles for the shoulders and elbows. Draw a half triangle for the hands together.

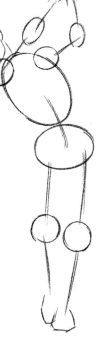

3 Sketch a small oval for the head. Add a short vertical line for the back of the neck. Sketch guidelines for the eyes, nose, and mouth. Draw the hands. Add two lines coming to a point for the golf club **shaft.** Add a rounded triangle shape for the **head** of the club.

4 Fill in the shape of the body by drawing lines connecting the guideline circles. Draw a line across the waist.

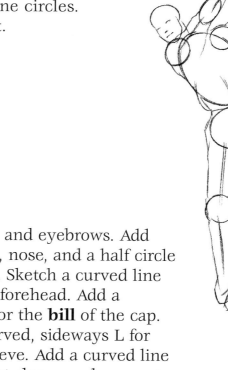

5 Draw eyes and eyebrows. Add the mouth, nose, and a half circle for the ear. Sketch a curved line across the forehead. Add a **crescent** for the **bill** of the cap. Draw a curved, sideways L for the left sleeve. Add a curved line for the right sleeve and connect it to the shirt. Draw the belt and add lines for pleated pants.

6 Erase the guidelines you no longer need. Darken the lines of the drawing. Color the hat. Add **shading** along the arms and face, and to the sleeves and shirt. Draw vertical lines in the pants and shirt to show folds. Add shading around Tiger's feet for a shadow.

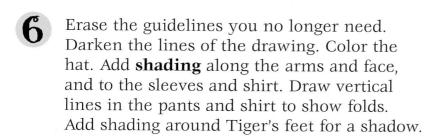

Glossary

bill front of a baseball-type hat that shades the wearer's eyes from the sun

blade bottom part of an ice skate

commercial artist person who designs and illustrates things for other people

crescent curved line that narrows to points at either end

dribbling moving down the field with a soccer ball by kicking the ball a little bit at a time

facemask mask that fits on the front of a helmet and protects the wearer's face

forearm part of the arm below the elbow

head part of a golf club that is used to hit the ball

jersey type of shirt worn by athletes

prodigy child or young person who is extremely talented

puck round piece of black rubber used like a ball in hockey

retired in sports, when a team retires a player's number nobody else can ever wear that number

seam line that is created where two pieces of material come together

shaft pole part of a golf club

temple side of the forehead